New Birth

Kenneth E. Hagin

Therefore if any man be in Christ, *he is a new creature* (i.e. creation): *old things are passed away; behold, all things are become new.*

—2 Corinthians 5:17

"It's not important what church you are in. The important thing is: What family are you in?"

CHAPTER 1

Born Again . . . Into the Family of God

The key which unlocks all the promises of God is this—Jesus taught that a man must be born again. The following statements came from the lips of Jesus:

"*. . . Except a man be born again, he cannot see the kingdom of God*" (John 3:3).

"*. . . Except a man be born of water and of the Spirit, he cannot enter into the kingdom of God*" (John 3:5).

"*. . . Except ye be converted, and become as little children, ye shall not enter into the kingdom of heaven*" (Matt. 18:3).

"*. . . except ye repent, ye shall all likewise perish*" (Luke 13:3,5).

The New Birth is a necessity to being saved. Through the New Birth you come into the right relationship to God. The New Birth is necessary before you can claim any of the benefits of the Bible.

The New Birth is not: confirmation—church membership—water baptism—the taking of sacraments—observing religious duties—an intellectual reception of Christianity—orthodoxy of faith—going to church—saying prayers—reading the Bible—being moral—being cultured or refined—doing good deeds—doing your best—nor any of the many other things some men are trusting in to save them.

Nicodemus, whom Jesus addressed concerning the New Birth, possessed most of the qualities we just listed, but Jesus said to him, *"Ye must be born again"* (John 3:7).

The thief on the cross, and others Jesus forgave while on earth, were saved without these things. They simply did the one necessary thing—they accepted Jesus Christ as personal Savior by repenting and turning to God with the whole heart as a little child.

One who is born again will automatically have the external evidences of a good life by virtue of the New Birth. But there are millions, it is sad to say, who are trusting in good works to save them. And millions will die and be lost without the New Birth because they have been misled concerning the experience of being born again.

It is all important that we pay personal attention to our eternal welfare—and that we not trust the best of men in the matter. If we permit men to mislead us in eternal matters and are lost—it will be too late to personally see after our welfare. Do something about it now.

Don't take the attitude that you cannot be deceived. Don't take the attitude that your church is the only right one and that it cannot mislead you. Your church may be right in its teaching concerning the New Birth. But make certain by going to the Bible yourself, and seeing with your own eyes, and knowing with your own heart—that you are right with God—that you have the real New Birth—and that you are living right with God every day.

There is no purpose served in fooling yourself. You are either born again—or you are not. You are either really saved—or you are being deceived into thinking you are, and you are lost.

You know your own life and your true relationship to God. So get the facts settled that you are a genuinely saved person, and in present contact with God.

Culture, refinement, and outward correctness of life—in the organized church or out of it—cannot take the place of the New Birth. For the trouble, you see, is in the heart.

Jesus said, *"For from within, out of the heart of men, proceed evil thoughts, adulteries, fornications, murders, Thefts, covetousness, wickedness, deceit, lasciviousness, an evil eye, blasphemy, pride, foolishness: All these evil things come from within, and defile the man"* (Mark 7:21–23).

The trouble is in the heart, the inward man, the spirit. Merely to reform the outward man or the outward life will not save you.

An artist could put a beautifully colored coating of wax on the outside of a rotten apple—but the apple would still be rotten at heart. One bite into it would be a bite into decay.

Out of Christ, every man is rotten in the heart. And mere outward correctness of life, apart from Christ, is artificial and the practice of hypocrites. And Jesus said of those He called hypocrites, *". . . for ye are like unto whited sepulchres, which indeed appear beautiful outward, but are within full of dead men's bones, and of all uncleanness"* (Matt. 23:27).

CHAPTER 2

From Death Unto Life

The Bible is a mystery book until we find the key that opens it. Then it ceases to be a mystery and becomes a message. There are two words which open up the Bible to our understanding—and those words are *life* and *death*.

Death has been a mystery in all ages. Science stands utterly mute in its presence, unable to explain it. Philosophy turns poetical when it meets this dread enemy of man. And theology has dealt only in generalities when attempting to explain it.

Death, that bloodhound-like foe, began its work at the cradle of the human race, and has followed the human race down through the stream of the centuries until the present hour. Death was not a part of the Creation, nor a part of God's original plan. Even physical death is an enemy of God and an enemy of man. The Bible says in First Corinthians 15:26 that physical death is the last enemy that shall be put under foot.

Before we can understand the nature of death, however, we must understand the nature of man. Man is not a physical being. Man is a spirit. In fact, man is a *spirit*, who possesses a *soul*, and lives in a *body* (1 Thess. 5:23).

When Jesus told Nicodemus, *"Ye must be born again"* (John 3:7), Nicodemus was thinking naturally and he asked, *"How can a man be born when he is old? Can he enter the second time into his mother's womb, and be born?"* And Jesus explained, *"That which is born of the flesh is flesh; and that which is born of the Spirit is spirit"* (John 3:4,6).

The New Birth is the rebirth of the human spirit.

The real man is spirit. The spirit operates through the soul (man's intellect, emotions, and will). And the soul in turn operates through the physical body.

Now the man (who is spirit) and his soul live in a physical body. At physical death, the

8

man and his soul leave the physical body and go to their eternal home.

Christ gave us in Luke 16:19–24 the experience of the rich man and Lazarus.

LUKE 16:19–24

19 There was a certain rich man, which was clothed in purple and fine linen, and fared sumptuously every day:

20 And there was a certain beggar named Lazarus, which was laid at his gate, full of sores,

21 And desiring to be fed with the crumbs which fell from the rich man's table: moreover the dogs came and licked his sores.

22 And it came to pass, that the beggar died [physically], and was carried by the angels into Abraham's bosom [Notice the angels carried him—not his body—but him, spirit and soul, to Abraham's bosom.]: the rich man also died, and was buried;

23 And in hell he lifted up his eyes, being in torments, and seeth Abraham afar off, and Lazarus in his bosom.

24 And he cried and said, Father Abraham, have mercy on me, and send Lazarus, that he may dip the tip of his finger in water, and cool my tongue; for I am tormented in this flame.

Lazarus and the rich man were still conscious. Man is not dead like an animal as some folks would have you believe. And there is no such thing as soul sleep.

Several kinds of deaths are spoken of in the Bible, but there are three kinds with which we need to familiarize ourselves: 1) Spiritual Death, 2) Physical Death, 3) Eternal Death, or the Second Death, which is being cast into the lake which burneth with fire and brimstone.

Spiritual death came to the earth first, then manifested itself in the physical body by destroying it. Physical death is but a manifestation of the law which is at work within, called by Paul, *"the law of sin and death"* (Romans 8:2).

When God said to Adam, "In the day that thou eatest thereof thou shalt surely die," He did not refer to physical death, but to spiritual death. If man had never died spiritually, he would not have died physically.

Spiritual death means separation from God. The moment Adam sinned, he was separated from God. And when God came down in the cool of the day, as was His custom to walk and talk with Adam, and called, "Adam, where art thou?" Adam said, "I hid myself." He was separated from God.

Man is now united with the devil. He is an outcast, an outlaw, driven from the garden with no legal ground of approach to God. He no longer responds to the call of God. He responds only to his new nature, or to his new master. Man is more than a transgressor. He is more than a law-breaker and a sinner. Man is spiritually a child of the devil and he partakes of his father's nature.

This explains why man cannot be saved by conduct. He has to be born again. If man were not a child of the devil, then he could just begin to put on the right kind of conduct, and he'd be all right. But even if he puts on right conduct, he's still a child of the devil, and will go to hell when he dies—to the lake which burneth with fire and brimstone, which is the second death.

Man cannot stand in the presence of God as he is—because he has the nature of his father, the devil, in him. If man is ever saved, he has to be saved by someone paying the penalty for his sins, and by someone giving him a new nature.

You might take a flop-eared mule and try to make a racehorse of him. You could file his teeth and polish his hooves. You could feed him the finest food, run him around the track every day, and house him in the finest stable. But on the day of the race when the gun sounds, all he'll do is lope off down the track—because he's a mule. It's just not in him. Yet you can take a racehorse, and not give him as good care, but when you put him on the starting line, and the gun sounds—he's gone! It's his nature. He's born and bred that way. In order for that old mule to be a racehorse, he would have to be reborn—and that's impossible.

Man, however, who is a spirit living in a body, can be reborn. His nature can be changed. He can become a new creature in Christ Jesus.

It doesn't matter how well-educated man becomes, how many degrees he has at the end of his name, how many dollars he has, how good a social worker he is, nor how religious he is—man cannot stand in the presence of God. His nature is wrong. Man is lost today, not because of what he does—but because of what he is. (What he does is the result of what he is.) Man needs *life* from God, because he is spiritually *dead.* Thanks be to God, Christ has redeemed us from spiritual death.

JOHN 5:26

26 For as the Father hath life in himself; so hath he given to the Son to have life in himself.

The new Man, Jesus Christ, had no death in Him. He was not born as we are born, and He didn't have the spiritual nature of death—the devil—in Him. Yet the Bible says in Hebrews 2:9 that He tasted death for every man.

Jesus Christ took upon Himself our sin nature. Hebrews 9:26 says He, "*. . . put away sin* [not sins] *by the sacrifice of himself.*" He took upon Himself our sin nature, the nature of spiritual death, that we might have Eternal Life.

Jesus said, *"The thief [the devil] cometh not, but for to steal, and to kill, and to destroy: I am come that they might have life, and that they might have it more abundantly"* (John 10:10).

He also said *". . . I say unto you, He that heareth my word, and believeth on him that sent me, hath everlasting life, and shall not come into condemnation; but is passed from death unto life"* (John 5:24).

Jesus came to redeem us from spiritual death! Adam was banished from the Tree of Life through rejecting God's Word. According to Revelation 2:7, all who now accept and obey the Word of God are brought back to the Tree of Life.

The New Birth does not take place gradually. It is instantaneous! It is a gift of God received the moment we believe.

In Ephesians 2:1 it says that you who were dead in trespasses and sins—that's spiritual death—He has quickened, made alive. And verses 8 and 9 tell you how it came about:

14

EPHESIANS 2:8–9

8   For by grace are ye saved through faith; and that not of yourselves: it is the gift of God:

9   Not of works, lest any man should boast.

Not of works! That punctures the balloon of the ego. Man wants to do something to save himself. He wants to have a part in it. But he can't.

You have to simply admit your helplessness—and your hopelessness. You have to admit that you are just what the Bible says—a lost sinner. Then you come and accept what Christ has wrought for you—a gift!

Have you passed from spiritual death unto spiritual life?

Is God your Father? Can you look up to heaven and say, "Father God"? Is His Spirit within your spirit bearing witness that you are a child of God? Do you have the Holy Spirit in your spirit crying, "Abba, Father"?

You do if you are born again. If you are not born again—accept Christ as your Savior today!

ROMANS 8:14–16

14 For as many as are led by the Spirit of God, they are the sons of God.

15 For ye have not received the spirit of bondage again to fear; but ye have received the Spirit of adoption, whereby we cry, Abba, Father.

16 The Spirit itself beareth witness with our spirit, that we are the children of God.

CHAPTER 3

The New Birth

Therefore if any man be in Christ, he is a new creature [creation]: *old things are passed away; behold, all things are become new.*

—2 Corinthians 5:17

The New Birth is a *new creation* from above—the direct operation of the Word of God and the Spirit of God upon your life—changing your spirit completely when you truly repent and turn to God. This *new creation* is brought about in the following manner:

- Recognize that you are a sinner, lost, without God, and without hope (Rom. 3:23).
- Admit that Jesus Christ died on the cross to save you from sin by His own precious blood.
- Come to God, turning away from sin and confessing Jesus as your Lord—*and you shall*

be born again. (The Holy Spirit will then make you a new creature—a new creation—cleansing you from all sin by the authority of the Word of God and by the blood of Christ which was shed to atone for your sin.)

- Believe from your heart and confess with your mouth that God does forgive you of your sins and that you are born again.

Believe and Confess

Here are some Scriptures which show you what you have in your authority to believe and to confess:

ROMANS 10:9-10

9 That if thou shalt confess with thy mouth the Lord Jesus, and shalt believe in thine heart that God hath raised him from the dead, thou shalt be saved.

10 For with the heart man believeth unto righteousness; and with the mouth confession is made unto salvation.

JOHN 1:12-13

12 But as many as received him, to them gave he power to become the sons of God, even to them that believe on his name:

13 Which were born, not of blood, nor of the will of the flesh, nor of the will of man, but of God.

JOHN 6:37

37 . . . and him that cometh to me I will in no wise cast out.

Oh, what a basis for faith! There is no such thing as a person coming to Him and being cast out! Jesus said, *". . . him that cometh to me I will in no wise cast out."*

JOHN 3:14–21

14 And as Moses lifted up the serpent in the wilderness, even so must the Son of man be lifted up:

15 That whosoever believeth in him should not perish, but have eternal life.

16 For God so loved the world, that he gave his only begotten Son, that whosoever believeth in him should not perish, but have everlasting life.

17 For God sent not his Son into the world to condemn the world; but that the world through him might be saved.

18 He that believeth on him is not condemned: but he that believeth not is condemned already, because he hath not believed in the name of the only begotten Son of God.

19 And this is the condemnation, that light is come into the world, and men loved darkness rather than light, because their deeds were evil.

20 For every one that doeth evil hateth the light, neither cometh to the light, lest his deeds should be reproved.

21 But he that doeth truth cometh to the light, that his deeds may be made manifest, that they are wrought in God.

JOHN 3:36

36 He that believeth on the Son hath everlasting life: and he that believeth not the Son shall not see life; but the wrath of God abideth on him.

JOHN 5:24

24 Verily, verily, I say unto you, He that heareth my word, and believeth on him that sent me, hath everlasting life, and shall not come into condemnation; but is passed from death unto life.

ACTS 3:19

19 Repent ye therefore, and be converted, that your sins may be blotted out, when the times of refreshing shall come from the presence of the Lord.

EPHESIANS 2:8–9

8 For by grace are ye saved through faith; and that not of yourselves: it is the gift of God:

9 Not of works, lest any man should boast.

You have the intelligence to see for yourself what the Bible says. Again we warn—do not listen to the interpretations of men who will tear apart the simple Scriptures and leave you confused.

They do not care for your soul or they would not seek to rob you of your true Christian experiences. If they had a love for you at all, they would at least permit you to believe the Bible just as it is. And they would encourage you to get Bible experiences.

When they fight so hard to rob you of these benefits, you would be a fool not to wake up and see that they are agents of the devil in sending men to hell. It matters not that they are the most refined and wonderful religious men you have ever met—they are not ministers of God if they are robbing you of God's blessing.

The Bible says, *"And no marvel; for Satan himself is transformed into an angel of light. Therefore it is no great thing if his ministers also be transformed as the ministers of righteousness; whose end shall be according to their works"* (2 Cor. 11:14–15).

CHAPTER 4

The Water of
the New Birth

We read that Jesus said, *"Marvel not that I said unto thee, Ye must be born again"* (John 3:7). Just before He said that, Jesus said, *". . . Verily, verily, I say unto thee, Except a man be born of water and of the Spirit, he cannot enter into the kingdom of God"* (John 3:5).

What is the *water* of the New Birth? What does this water of the New Birth mean?

Does it refer to being baptized in water? Does that save you? No, that is not what Jesus is talking about.

The Word of God is the water referred to in John 3:5. Let's prove that by looking through a number of Scriptures.

EPHESIANS 5:26
26 That he might sanctify and cleanse it [the church] with the washing of water by the word.

JOHN 6:63

63 It is the spirit that quickeneth; the flesh profiteth nothing: the words that I speak unto you, they are spirit, and they are life.

JOHN 15:3

3 Now ye are clean through the word which I have spoken unto you.

JOHN 17:17

17 Sanctify them through thy truth: thy word is truth.

1 PETER 1:23

23 Being born again, not of corruptible seed, but of incorruptible, by the word of God, which liveth and abideth for ever.

JAMES 1:18

18 Of his own will begat he us with the word of truth, that we should be a kind of firstfruits of his creatures.

One must believe what the Word of God says about man—that man is a sinner and that Christ died to save him from all sin. Then if man will confess his sins to God and turn from sin with a whole heart and believe the Gospel—he is conforming to the Word of God.

The Holy Spirit will then transform his life by the power of the Word of God and by the blood of Christ. That moment—he is born again!

This new creation—the newly born child of God—is then to believe the Word of God and walk accordingly. He must begin to read the Bible and pray to God. He needs to walk and live in the spirit and be conformed to the Word of God as he receives light.

Being born again—becoming the child of God—is of foremost importance. It is the key that unlocks all the promises of God to you. For when you become a child of God—then God's promises becomes yours.

CHAPTER 5

New Creation Facts

Believers, Christians—here are some Bible facts about the *new creation* you are in Christ:

You Are a Child of God

No truth in all the Bible is as far reaching as the blessed fact that when we are born again into the family of God—*God the Father is our Father*. He cares for us! He is interested in us—each of us individually—not just as a group, or as a body or a church. He is interested in each of His children and loves each one of us with the same love.

Much is heard about the *fatherhood* of God and the *brotherhood* of man, but Jesus said to some very religious people, "You are of your father the devil" (John 8:44). God is the Creator of all mankind, but a man must be born again to become His child. He is God to the world, but Father only to the new creation man.

God is your very own Father. You are His very own child. And if He is your Father, you can be assured He will take a father's place and perform a father's part. You can be certain that as your Father He loves you, and will take care of you. (See John 14:23; John 16:23,27; Matt. 6:8–9,26, 30–34; Matt. 7:11.)

Get acquainted with your Father through the Word. When you were saved, you were born into His family as a spiritual baby. Babies in the natural must eat natural food to develop and grow. The Bible instructs the children of God: *"As newborn babes, desire the sincere milk of the word, that ye may grow thereby . . ."* (1 Peter 2:2). It is in the Word where we find out about our Father, about His love, His nature, how He cares for us, and how He loves us. He is everything the Word says He is. He will do everything the Word says He will do.

You Are a New Creature— A New Creation—A New Species

I'm glad I am a new creature. I was only 15, but I remember when it happened. Something took place inside of me. It seemed as if a two-ton load rolled off my chest. Not only did something depart from me—but something came into me. I was not the same person. There was a change inside.

In the New Birth, our spirits are recreated. (Our bodies are not. It is in our spirit where all things have become new. We still have the same bodies we always had.) There is a man who lives inside the body. Paul calls him the *inward man*. (He calls the body the *outward man*.)

2 CORINTHIANS 4:16

16 . . . but though our outward man perish, yet the inward man is renewed day by day.

Peter calls this inner man *the hidden man of the heart* (1 Peter 3:4). This man is hidden to the physical eye. No one can see the real you— the inward man. They may think they do but they only see the house (the body) you live in. You are on the inside looking out. The same thing is true with the people you know: you've never really seen the real man on the inside. You don't know what he looks like. You have only seen the house they live in. When a man's house is decayed, the real man still lives. The real man never dies.

It is this inward man who becomes a new man in Christ. A new creation. It is the inward man who is born into the family of God—who is God's own child—and who is in perfect union with the Master.

You Are One With the Master

1 CORINTHIANS 6:17

17 But he that is joined unto the Lord is one spirit.

The believer and Jesus are one. Jesus said, "*I am the vine, ye are the branches . . .*" (John 15:5). When you look at a tree you don't think of the branches as one part, and the rest of the tree as another part. You see it as one—as a unity. We are one with Christ. Our spirits are one with Him. Jesus is the head—we are the body.

All Things Are Possible to You

No one argues with the Scripture which says, ". . . *with God all things are possible*" (Matt. 19:26). Yet the same New Testament also says, ". . . *all things are possible to him that believeth*" (Mark 9:23).

Are these Scriptures equally true? Could one be a statement of fact and the other a misconception? A falsehood? No! Both statements are fact.

All things are possible to him that believeth. It helps me as I drive down the road to say that. It helps me when I face a seemingly impossible situation to say aloud, "All things are possible to him that believeth. And I believe!"

The Greater One Is in You

1 JOHN 4:4

4 Ye are of God, little children, and have overcome them: because greater is he that is in you,
than he that is in the world.

"Ye are of God. . . ."

This is another way of saying you are born of God. It says the same thing Second Corinthians 5:17 says: that if any man be in Christ he is a new creation. John is telling us we are born of God, that we have been born again, that *our spirits have been recreated*, that we are *of God*.

Sadly, many Christians don't know they are born of God—and that they have received Eternal Life (the life and nature of God). They think Eternal Life is something they are "going to have" when they get to heaven. Many think they have simply received forgiveness of sins.

If we have just been taught that our sins are forgiven and that we will remain justified only if we walk carefully before God—and we have never been taught that the nature of God is within our spirits—then sin and Satan will continue to reign over us.

But when we know that the man on the inside, the real man, has been *born again* and is a *new self* in Christ Jesus—then we will rule and reign over Satan.

"Ye are of God, little children, and have overcome them: because greater is he that is in you, than he that is in the world" (1 John 4:4).

He that is in the world is the god of this world—Satan (2 Cor. 4:4). But thank God, greater is He who is in us than the god of this

30

world! Greater is He that is in us than Satan. He that is in us is greater than demons. He is greater than evil spirits. He is greater than sickness. He is greater than disease. He is the Greater One! And He lives in me! He lives in you! He that is *in you* is greater than any force you may come against.

2 CORINTHIANS 6:16

16 . . . for ye are the temple of the living God; as God hath said, I will dwell in them, and walk in them; and I will be their God, and they shall be my people.

How many Christians are conscious of the fact that God is dwelling in them? It sounds far-fetched. But what does this Scripture mean if it does not mean what it says?

It is time for the Church to become "God-inside" minded. Too long it has been weakness-minded, sickness-minded, inferiority-complex-minded, trouble-and-poverty-minded. That's all we've talked and thought about until a serious condition of doubt, unbelief, and spiritual failure has been created in the church. This psychology of unbelief has robbed us of vibrant Christian faith and living, and of the abundant life Jesus intended that we should have.

JOHN 10:10

10 . . . I am come that they might have life, and that they might have it more abundantly.

When we know that the Life-Giver indwells us—that the Author of all life everywhere has condescended in the Person of His Son, through the power of the Holy Spirit, to come down and live within us—then our very beings shall radiate *Life!*

"Greater is He that is in you than he that is in the world." Grasp that. You are of God. You are born from above. The same mighty Spirit who raised Christ from the dead dwells in you. It's no wonder the Bible says, ". . . *all things are possible to him that believeth.*" It is because the God with whom all things are possible lives within us!